YELLOWSTONE
AND
GRAND TETON NATIONAL PARKS

An Activity Guide
By Daniel Ginsberg
Edited by Joyce G. Gellhorn

Roberts Rinehart, Inc. Publishers

for

TERRY LYNN and MARY SAGE

Copyright © 1990 by Daniel Ginsberg
Published by Roberts Rinehart, Inc. Publishers
Box 666 Niwot, Colorado 80544-0666
ISBN 0-911797-79-3
Printed in the United States of America

MY YELLOWSTONE-GRAND TETON ADVENTURE

This page is at the very beginning because it is a most important page.
It is for your thoughts about what you do and what you see during your
stay in Yellowstone and Grand Teton National Parks.

WHAT HAVE I SEEN?

WILDLIFE   **NATURAL WONDERS**

_____   _____

_____   _____

_____   _____

_____   _____

_____   _____

_____   _____

_____   _____

My adventure began _____ and ended _____

I think these parks are important because _____

_____

_____

I can help take care of these parks by _____

_____

_____

My most exciting moment was _____

_____

_____

_____

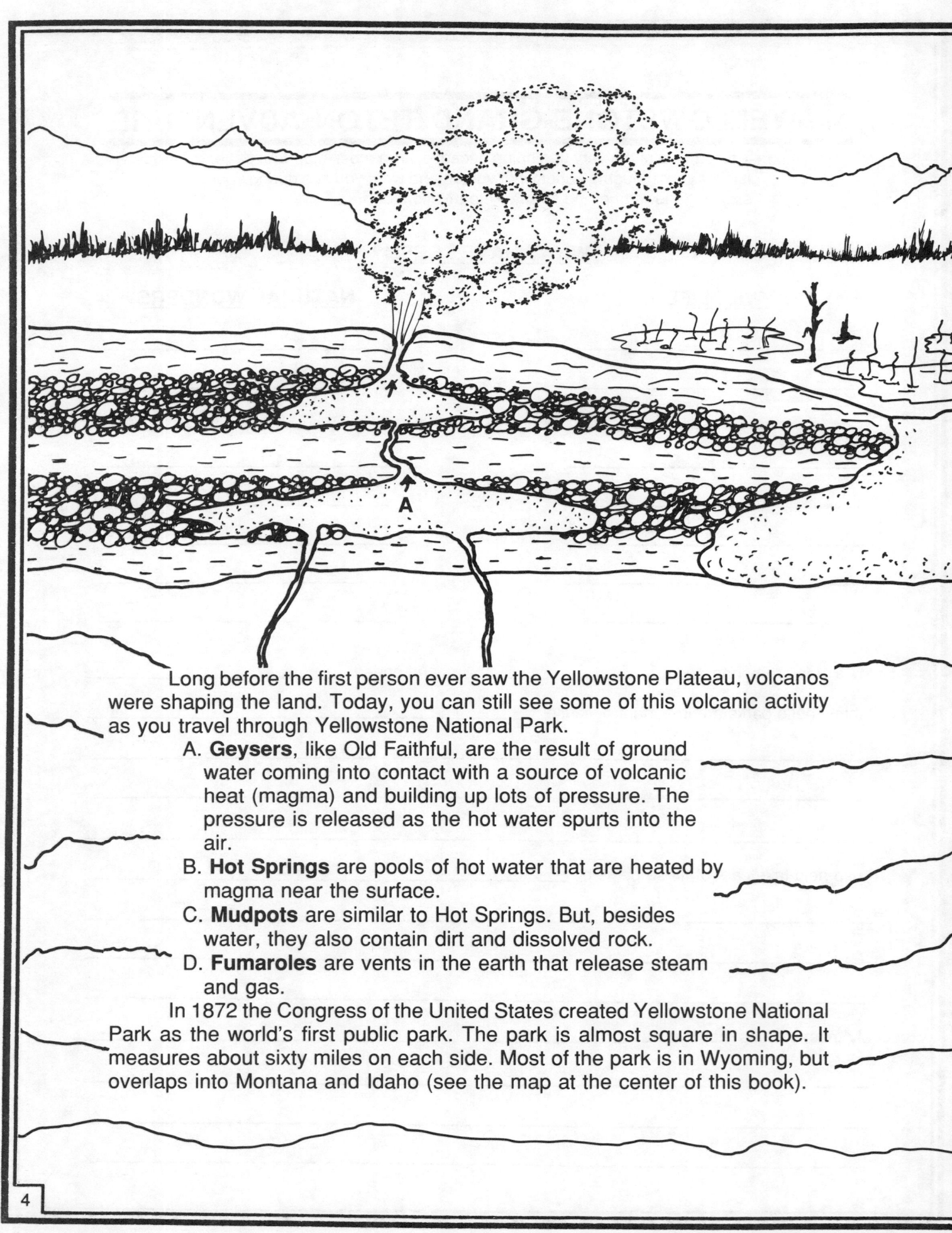

Long before the first person ever saw the Yellowstone Plateau, volcanos were shaping the land. Today, you can still see some of this volcanic activity as you travel through Yellowstone National Park.

A. **Geysers**, like Old Faithful, are the result of ground water coming into contact with a source of volcanic heat (magma) and building up lots of pressure. The pressure is released as the hot water spurts into the air.

B. **Hot Springs** are pools of hot water that are heated by magma near the surface.

C. **Mudpots** are similar to Hot Springs. But, besides water, they also contain dirt and dissolved rock.

D. **Fumaroles** are vents in the earth that release steam and gas.

In 1872 the Congress of the United States created Yellowstone National Park as the world's first public park. The park is almost square in shape. It measures about sixty miles on each side. Most of the park is in Wyoming, but overlaps into Montana and Idaho (see the map at the center of this book).

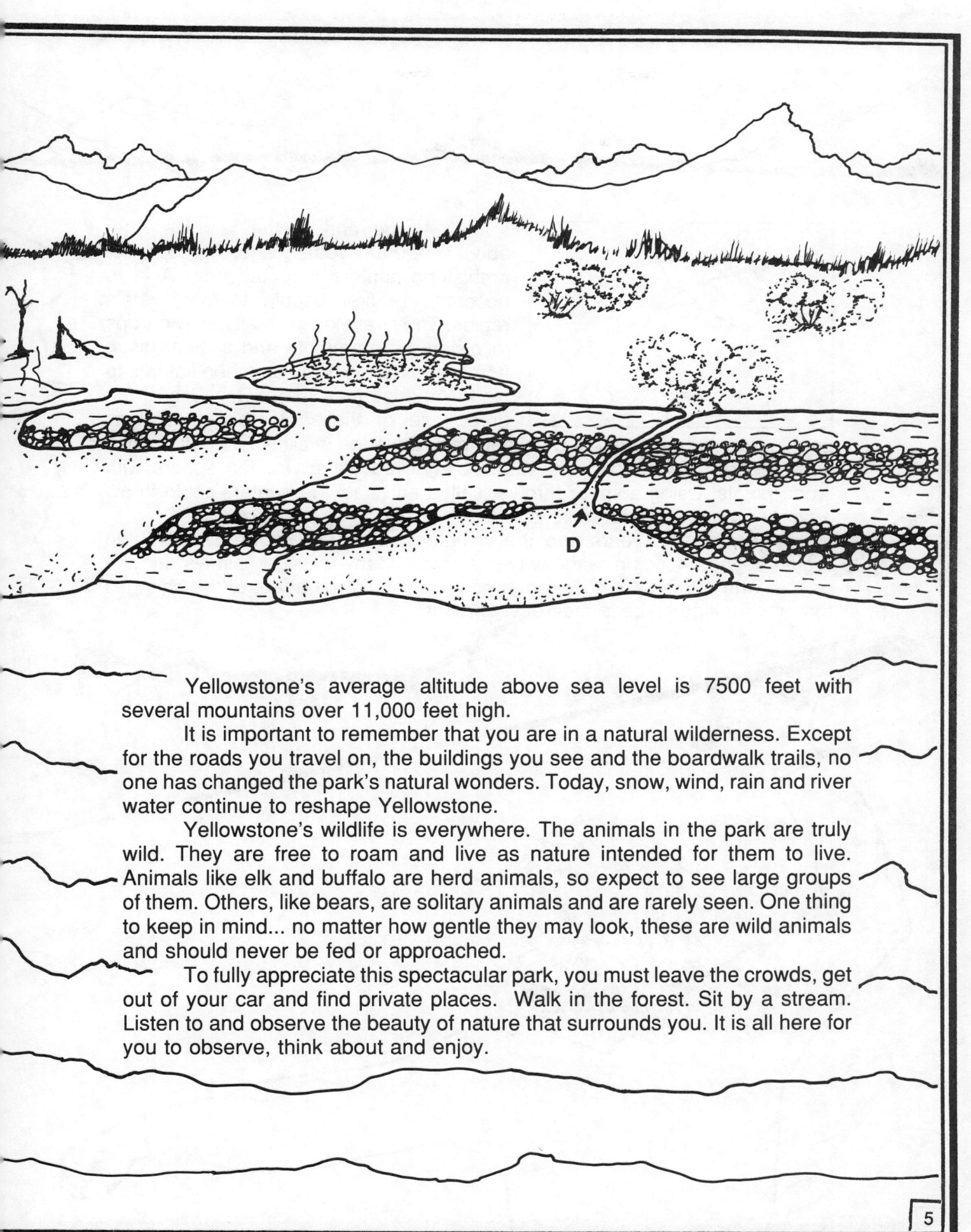

Yellowstone's average altitude above sea level is 7500 feet with several mountains over 11,000 feet high.

It is important to remember that you are in a natural wilderness. Except for the roads you travel on, the buildings you see and the boardwalk trails, no one has changed the park's natural wonders. Today, snow, wind, rain and river water continue to reshape Yellowstone.

Yellowstone's wildlife is everywhere. The animals in the park are truly wild. They are free to roam and live as nature intended for them to live. Animals like elk and buffalo are herd animals, so expect to see large groups of them. Others, like bears, are solitary animals and are rarely seen. One thing to keep in mind... no matter how gentle they may look, these are wild animals and should never be fed or approached.

To fully appreciate this spectacular park, you must leave the crowds, get out of your car and find private places. Walk in the forest. Sit by a stream. Listen to and observe the beauty of nature that surrounds you. It is all here for you to observe, think about and enjoy.

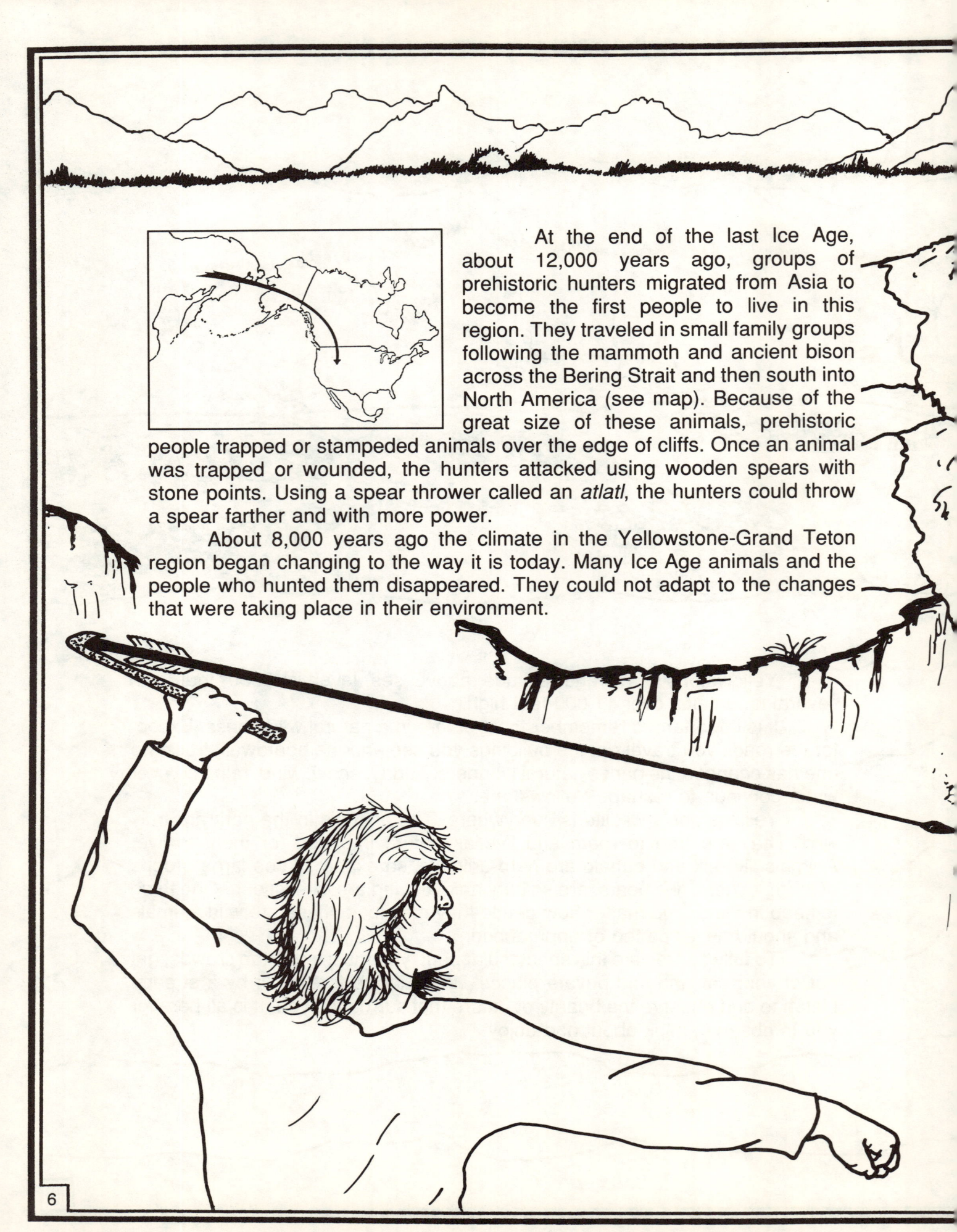

At the end of the last Ice Age, about 12,000 years ago, groups of prehistoric hunters migrated from Asia to become the first people to live in this region. They traveled in small family groups following the mammoth and ancient bison across the Bering Strait and then south into North America (see map). Because of the great size of these animals, prehistoric people trapped or stampeded animals over the edge of cliffs. Once an animal was trapped or wounded, the hunters attacked using wooden spears with stone points. Using a spear thrower called an *atlatl*, the hunters could throw a spear farther and with more power.

About 8,000 years ago the climate in the Yellowstone-Grand Teton region began changing to the way it is today. Many Ice Age animals and the people who hunted them disappeared. They could not adapt to the changes that were taking place in their environment.

Most of the Ice Age hunters were gone about 6,000 years ago. The people who could change and adapt to the new environment survived. They developed the bow and arrow and learned new ways to hunt. Using woven baskets and then pottery, they began storing roots, seeds, and berries. This allowed them to remain in one region instead of always having to follow animals as they roamed. Today, we call these people Native Americans. The Sheepeaters of the Shoshone Tribe lived in the Yellowstone area.

The Sheepeaters lived in peace until about 300 years ago. At that time, French fur trappers came into this region looking for beaver and other fur-bearing animals. Sadly, the peaceful way of life for Native Americans ended as more and more non-natives learned of this beautiful region and came out west.

Redraw each numbered box in the larger numbered box below.
Add your own background to the picture and have fun.

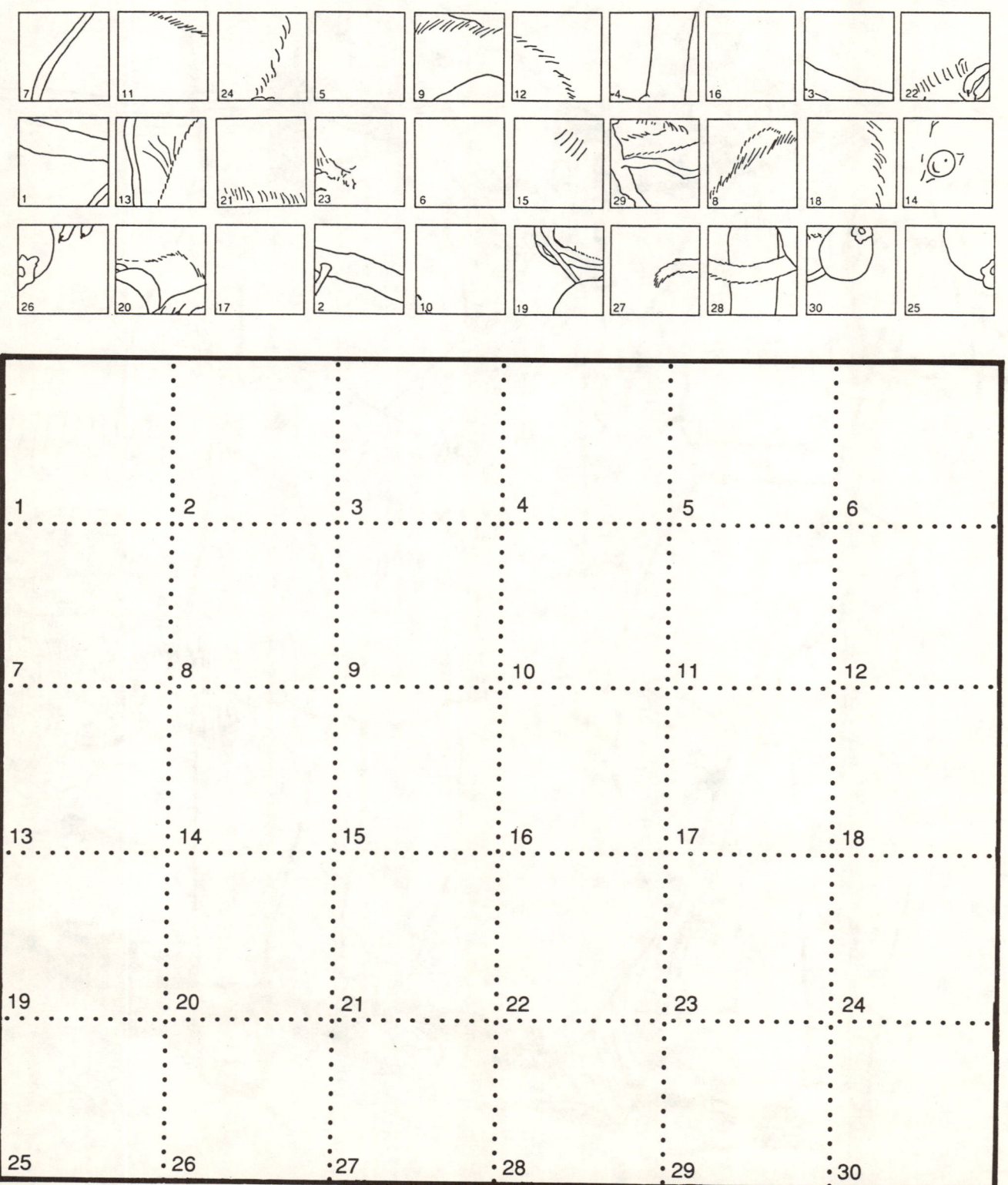

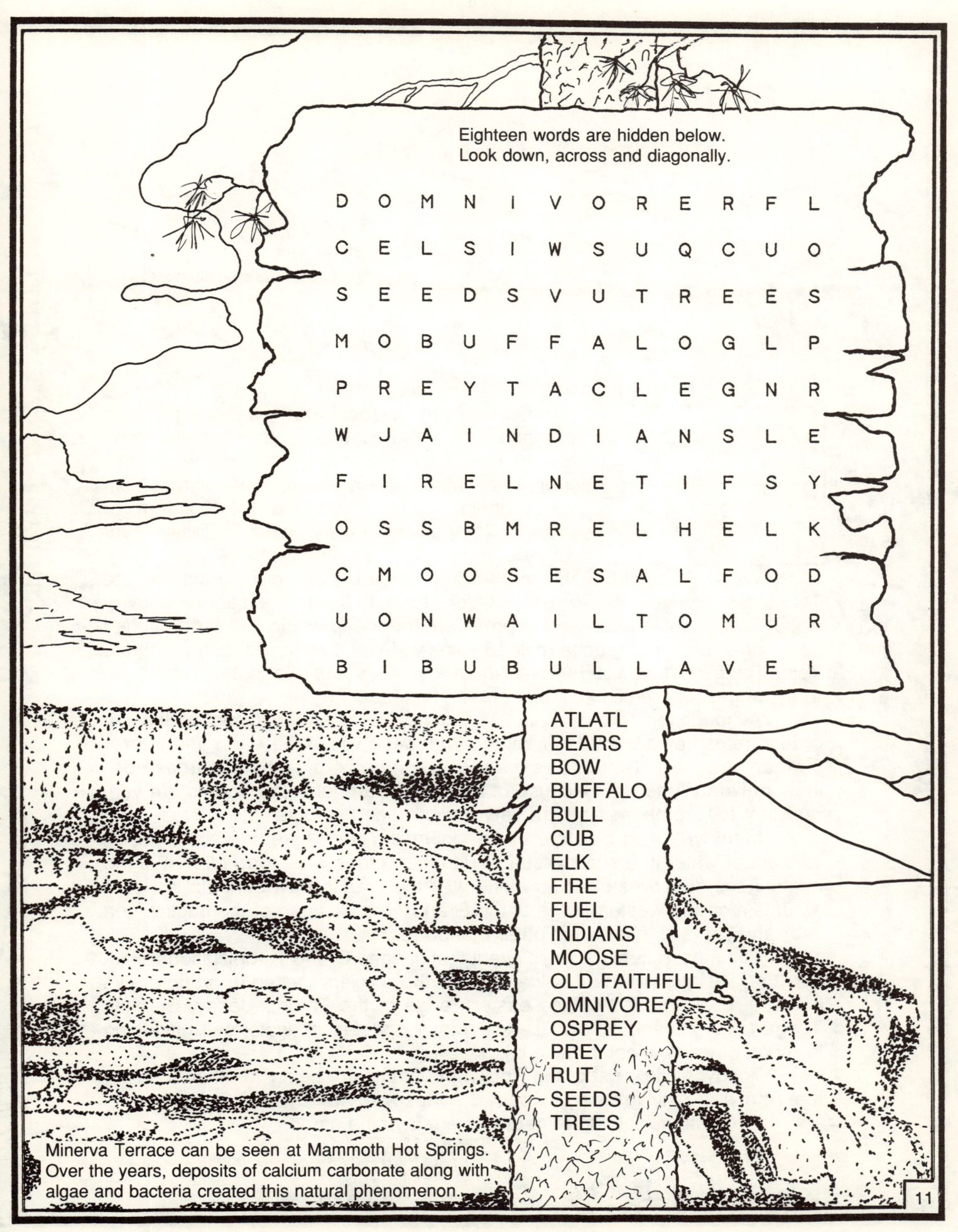

Eighteen words are hidden below.
Look down, across and diagonally.

```
D O M N I V O R E R F L
C E L S I W S U Q C U O
S E E D S V U T R E E S
M O B U F F A L O G L P
P R E Y T A C L E G N R
W J A I N D I A N S L E
F I R E L N E T I F S Y
O S S B M R E L H E L K
C M O O S E S A L F O D
U O N W A I L T O M U R
B I B U B U L L A V E L
```

ATLATL
BEARS
BOW
BUFFALO
BULL
CUB
ELK
FIRE
FUEL
INDIANS
MOOSE
OLD FAITHFUL
OMNIVORE
OSPREY
PREY
RUT
SEEDS
TREES

Minerva Terrace can be seen at Mammoth Hot Springs.
Over the years, deposits of calcium carbonate along with
algae and bacteria created this natural phenomenon.

Grand Teton National Park was established in 1929 and is located to the south of Yellowstone National Park (see the map in the center of this book). The Tetons are a sharp ridge of mountain peaks ranging from 11,000 to 14,000 feet in elevation. They are the tallest peaks in Snake River country.

While Yellowstone National Park was formed by volcanic activity, the Teton Range developed from a fault block formation (see the diagram above). About 9 million years ago, great pressure from deep within the earth pushed up a huge section of granite rock 15 miles wide by 40 miles long, forming the Teton Range. Would you believe that at 9 million years of age, the Tetons are the youngest of the Rocky Mountains? They are!

Although the Tetons are the newest portion of the Rocky Mountains, the granite rock they are made of comes from deep within the earth and is over 3 billion years old. That makes the rock some of the oldest and hardest rock in all of North America. Because of the rock's hardness, the Tetons are very resistant to weathering and are very steep rugged mountains.

Many years ago, before these mountains were here, the entire region was under water in a shallow sea. When the Tetons were formed, part of the original sea floor was tilted up along with the granite rock beneath it. Fossil Mountain on the western edge of the Grand Tetons is part of the original sea floor and contains shells and other marine fossils.

The most recent geologic event that shaped Grand Teton National Park was the glaciation of the last Ice Age. As the glaciers melted, a group of five beautiful lakes formed on the eastern edge of the Tetons: Jenny, Bradley, Taggart, Leigh, and Phelps Lakes. Many species of waterfowl, including trumpeter swans, inhabit these lakes.

Today, while most of the Rocky Mountains are being weathered down, the Tetons are still growing... about 6 inches every 300 years.

Remember, nothing in nature ever stays the same.

In 1912, the Congress of the United States began setting aside land for an elk refuge. Today, the 23,000 acre National Elk Refuge is located on the southeastern edge of Grand Teton National Park. About 8,000 elk spend the winter on the refuge.

In spring, the local Boy Scout Organization gathers all the naturally shed antlers they can find on the refuge. On the third Saturday in May the antlers are sold at a public auction in Jackson, Wyoming. The money from the sale aids local scouting and the winter feeding program on the National Elk Refuge.

Can you help the mouse in the middle
find a path out of all these antlers?

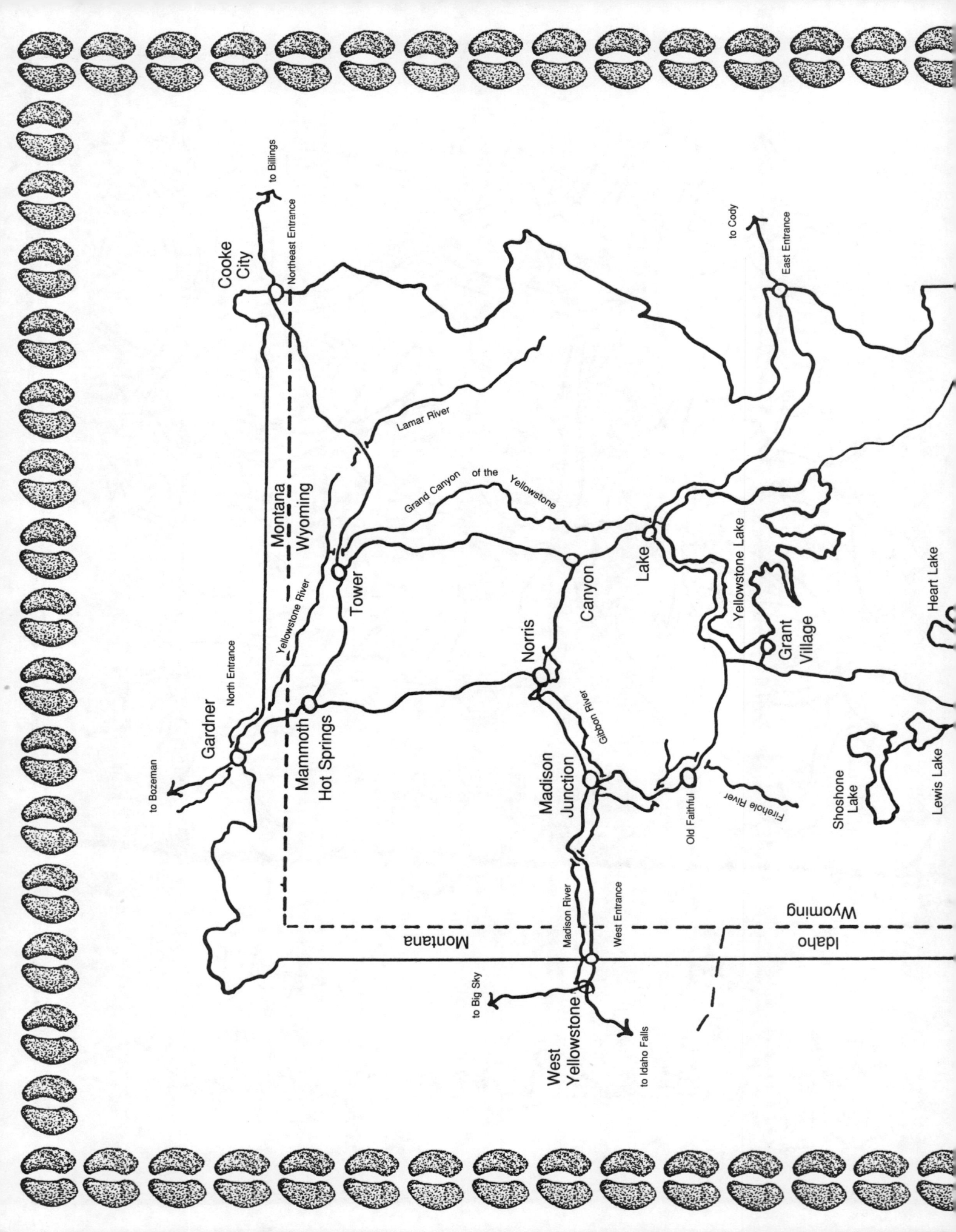

Yellowstone & Grand Teton National Parks

Snake River

South Entrance

to Dubois

Jackson Lake Junction

Moran Junction

Jackson Lake

Leigh Lake

Jenny Lake

Bradley Lake

Taggart Lake

Moose Village

Phelps Lake

Teton Range

to Jackson

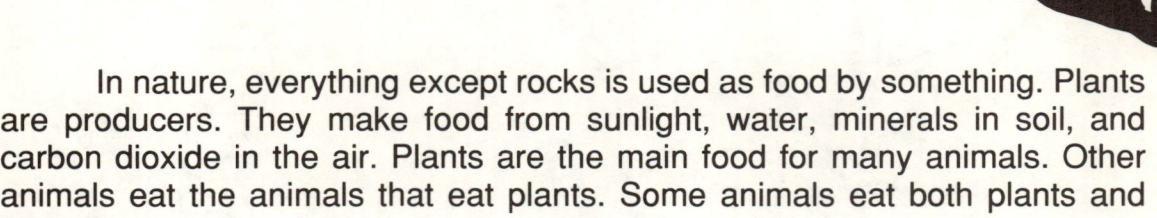

In nature, everything except rocks is used as food by something. Plants are producers. They make food from sunlight, water, minerals in soil, and carbon dioxide in the air. Plants are the main food for many animals. Other animals eat the animals that eat plants. Some animals eat both plants and animals.

A food chain describes what eats what. There are four main groups in a food chain:

-**Producers** are plants that make and store food.

-**Herbivores** are animals that eat plants. Beavers, elk, bighorn sheep and grasshoppers are only a few examples.

-**Carnivores** are meat eaters. The mountain lion, weasel and osprey (shown here) are predators: they kill the food they eat. Others, like vultures, are scavengers: they eat animals that are already dead. Bears, coyotes and bald eagles are both predators and scavengers.

-**Omnivores** eat both plants and animals. Bears are omnivores.

In which category of eaters do you belong?

Birds of prey, like this osprey, are proud, strong and fierce predators. Birds of prey are also called raptors. All raptors have sharp, hooked beaks and powerful feet. Their toes have sharp talons (claws) that are designed for grasping and holding flesh.

Raptors are sight hunters. They have especially keen eyesight, much sharper than humans do. This allows them to spot prey from over a mile away.

Every plant, animal, and insect is part of a food chain. Try to fit animals you know about into a food chain.

We have all been taught that fire kills. Many people feel that all fires should be put out as quickly as possible. This is true when fire endangers people or their homes. But, it is not always true where forests are concerned.

Fire has always been an important part of forests. Fires help forests remain healthy by clearing out dead trees and old undergrowth. This process returns needed nutrients to the soil. If small ground fires are permitted to burn, the large hot fires start only rarely.

In the summer of 1988 Yellowstone National Park experienced a series of large uncontrollable wildfires. It was one of the hottest driest summers ever. Most of these wildfires were started by lightning.

Now, as you walk along a nature trail, notice the new growth that is all around you.

Look closely and you will find new lodgepole pine seedlings in many fire scorched areas. Plants like the lodgepole pine actually need fire to help them release seeds from pine cones. New healthy grasses now grow where before there was only old undergrowth. This means more food for the park's animals and a better chance for survival.

Although the wildfires of 1988 were large and many acres were blackened, only a few small cabins were burned and very few animals were killed. Most animals simply moved out of the fire's path. The many acres that burned are not lost. They will continue to change as new plants grow and animals come back. Always remember, change is the way of nature.

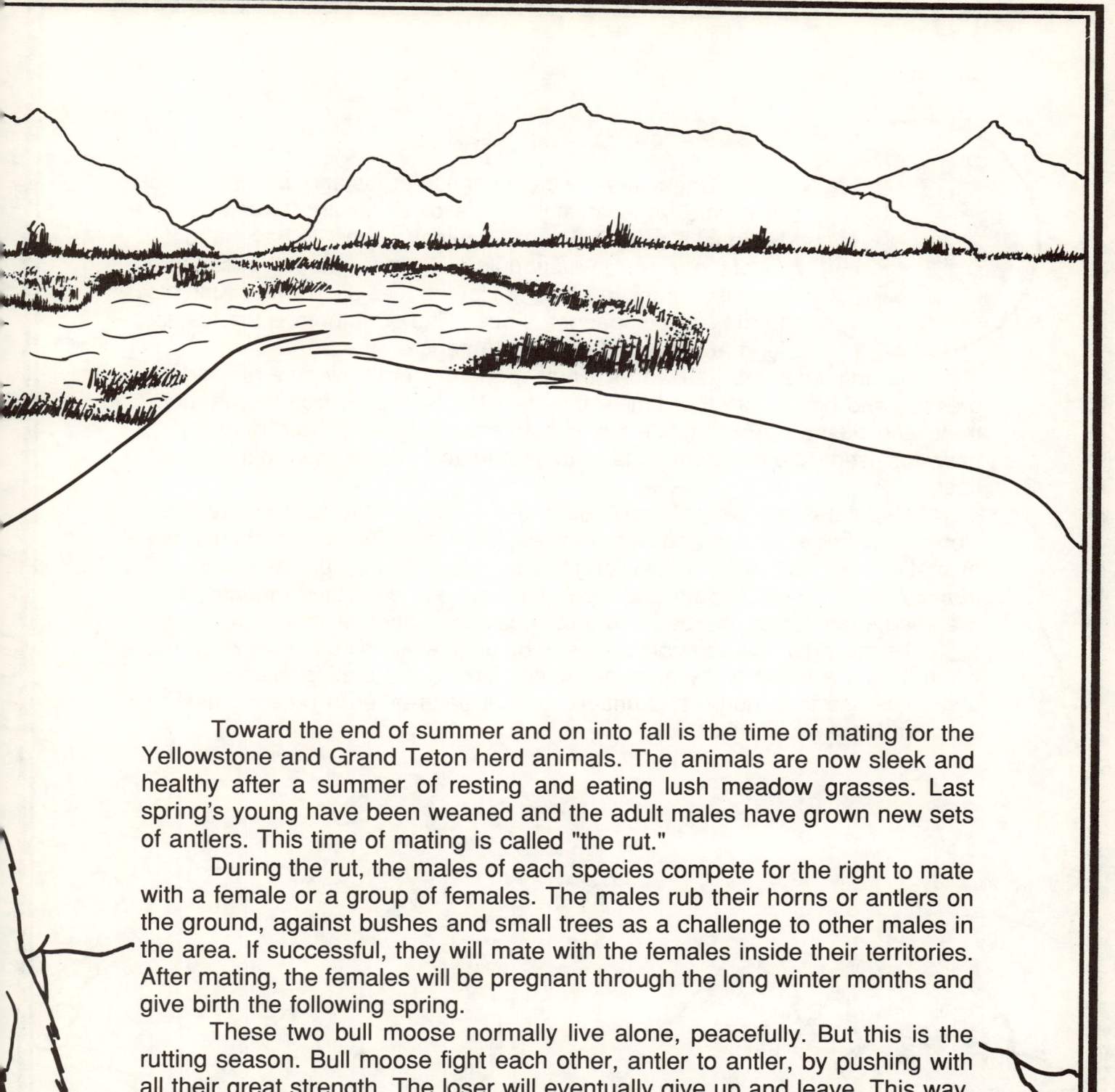

Toward the end of summer and on into fall is the time of mating for the Yellowstone and Grand Teton herd animals. The animals are now sleek and healthy after a summer of resting and eating lush meadow grasses. Last spring's young have been weaned and the adult males have grown new sets of antlers. This time of mating is called "the rut."

During the rut, the males of each species compete for the right to mate with a female or a group of females. The males rub their horns or antlers on the ground, against bushes and small trees as a challenge to other males in the area. If successful, they will mate with the females inside their territories. After mating, the females will be pregnant through the long winter months and give birth the following spring.

These two bull moose normally live alone, peacefully. But this is the rutting season. Bull moose fight each other, antler to antler, by pushing with all their great strength. The loser will eventually give up and leave. This way, few animals are injured and the loser can try again next year. Elk and deer use their antlers in the same way, just as bison and bighorn sheep use their heads and horns to fight.

Only the fittest and strongest males mate. In this way superior qualities are passed on to the offspring and a healthy herd is maintained. This is known as "survival of the fittest."

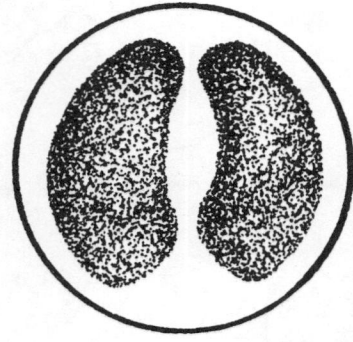

Ungulates are the most numerous and easiest to see of all the large animals in Yellowstone and Grand Teton National Parks. The word ungulate means "to have a hoof." All of the region's wild ungulates have two hoofed toes (note the bison track to the left). Hoofed toes allow these animals to run swiftly if danger is near. The pronghorn is the fastest land animal in all of North America.

All ungulates are herbivores. They spend most of their time grazing on grasses and herbs. At other times, they browse on leaves from a variety of trees and bushes. An ungulate's stomach is very different from ours. They have four separate compartments in their stomach to help them digest plant fiber.

Ungulates are the only animals in the world to have horns or antlers. Horns, like those of bison and bighorn sheep, are permanently attached to the animal's head and grow a little longer each year. Both the males and the females have horns. Antlers are grown by male elk, deer, and moose. They are shed each winter and begin to grow again in springtime.

Horns, antlers, and hoofs are used by ungulates as defensive weapons when they are attacked by another animal. During the mating season, male ungulates use their horns and antlers to fight each other in order to defend their territories.

The most misunderstood animal in North America is the wolf.

Wolves live and hunt together in a pack of 6 to 12 animals. All wolves in a pack cooperate while hunting. Cooperation allows the pack to hunt prey that would be too large for one animal to kill alone.

In the early spring, the dominant male of each pack mates with the dominant female. Six weeks later, a litter of pups are born in an underground den or cave. When the pups emerge from the den, the entire pack takes part in raising them.

Story books often show wolves as vicious killers. Most animals are pictured as good animals, while coyotes and wolves are shown to be bad. This kind of uninformed thinking caused the government to exterminate... kill... the last of this region's wolves during the 1920s.

Today we know that all animals are important in a balanced ecosystem. Each species does a job. Predators, such as wolves, prevent other species from overpopulating an area and depleting the food supply. Without predators, large numbers of animals like bison, elk, and deer die of starvation. Still, many people see the wolf only as a danger to domestic cattle and not as a benefit to the entire region.

What do you think? Should wolves be reintroduced into the Yellowstone ecosystem?

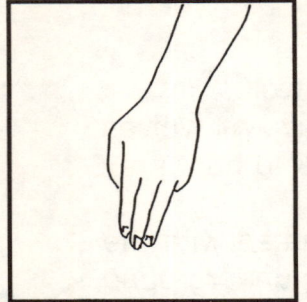 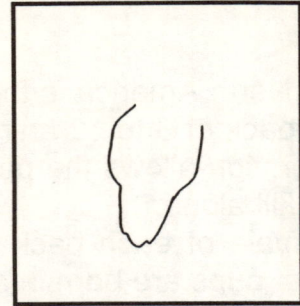  

Use these drawings as a guide to create your own picture. Have fun!

The bald eagle was chosen as our national
symbol because of its regal manner.

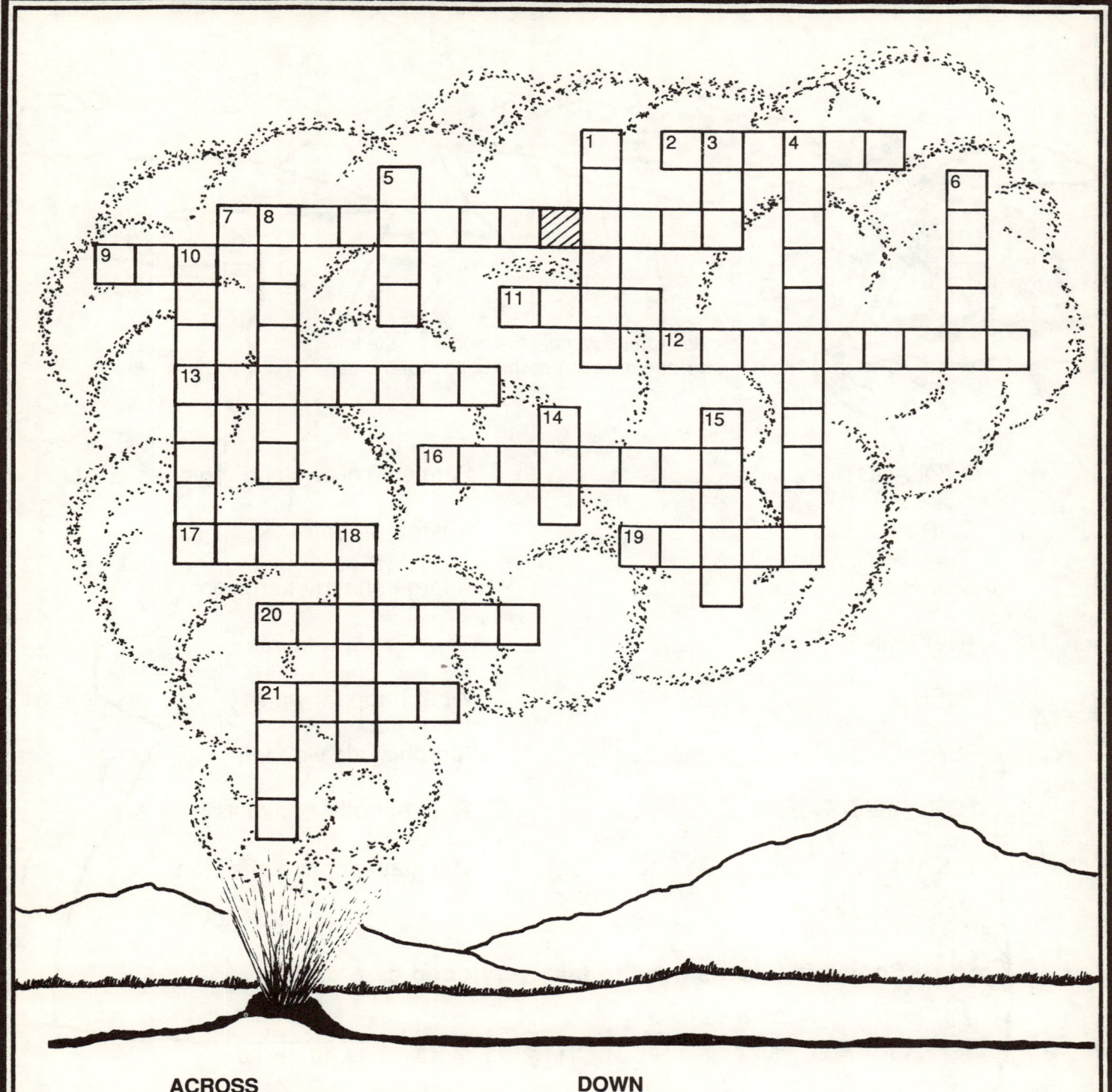

ACROSS

2. Sprays heated water into the air.
7. Yellowstone was the first one.
9. The ungulate mating season.
11. Animals that are eaten.
12. To be asleep for the winter.
13. Animals that hunt other animals.
16. An animal that has a hoof.
17. This comes out of fumeroles.
19. Used by bison during the rut.
20. Used a bow and arrow.
21. Yellowstone's tallest ungulate.

DOWN

1. A raptor.
3. An ungulate that bugles.
4. Yellowstone's only indians.
5. The most misunderstood predator.
6. The fish in Yellowstone lake.
8. Deer grow them every year.
10. People that hunt for furs.
14. Covers the skin of many animals.
15. Very large omnivores.
18. Formed by hot water and mud.
21. What carnivores eat.

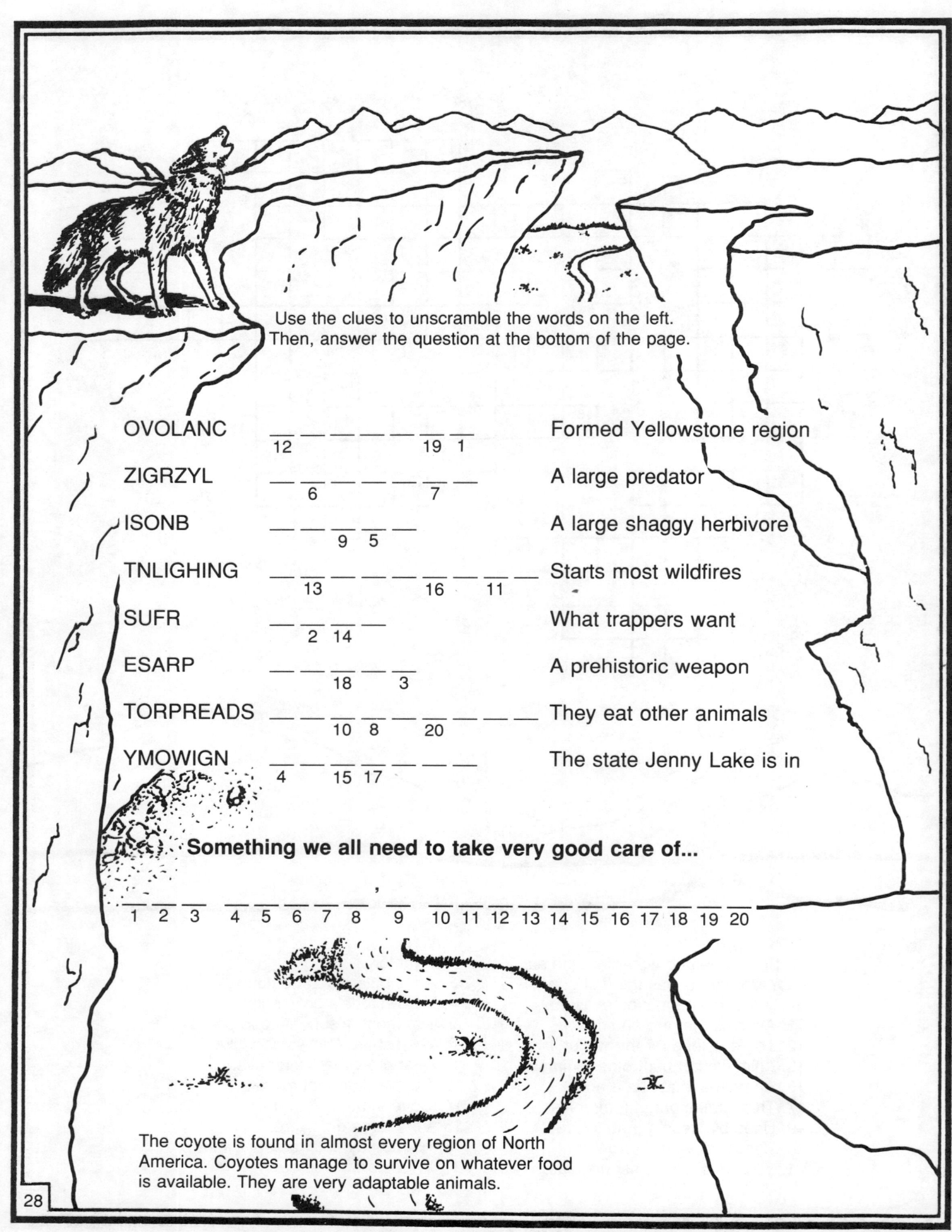

Use the clues to unscramble the words on the left.
Then, answer the question at the bottom of the page.

OVOLANC

___ ___ ___ ___ ___ ___ ___
12   19 1

Formed Yellowstone region

ZIGRZYL

___ ___ ___ ___ ___ ___ ___
     6   7

A large predator

ISONB

___ ___ ___ ___ ___
     9 5

A large shaggy herbivore

TNLIGHING

___ ___ ___ ___ ___ ___ ___ ___
13   16 11

Starts most wildfires

SUFR

___ ___ ___ ___
2 14

What trappers want

ESARP

___ ___ ___ ___ ___
18 3

A prehistoric weapon

TORPREADS

___ ___ ___ ___ ___ ___ ___ ___ ___
10 8   20

They eat other animals

YMOWIGN

___ ___ ___ ___ ___ ___ ___
4 15 17

The state Jenny Lake is in

Something we all need to take very good care of...

___ ___ ___ , ___ ___ ___ ___ ___ ___ ___ ___ ___ ___ ___ ___ ___ ___ ___ ___ ___
1 2 3   4 5 6 7 8   9   10 11 12 13 14 15 16 17 18 19 20

The coyote is found in almost every region of North
America. Coyotes manage to survive on whatever food
is available. They are very adaptable animals.

Fall is a season of change for the Yellowstone region. As the temperature drops, snow returns and covers the land. Animals must also change if they are to survive the cold snowy winter.

Many ungulates dig through the snow to find grass and shrubs to eat. Some animals find food on hillsides where wind has blown the snow away.

The coyote can no longer see mice or hear them rustling in the grass. During the winter, a coyote must use his keen sense of hearing to find his prey under the snow.

Other animals survive by avoiding much of the winter:
- Many species of birds fly south to warmer climates.
- Chipmunks, lizards, and frogs hibernate in nests or underground burrows. When an animal hibernates, its heart rate and breathing is very slow. Animals do not eat when they are hibernating.
- Bears do not really hibernate. They den up and spend most of the winter in a deep sleep. Many bears wake up and leave their dens for short periods of time during the winter.

How do you protect yourself during the cold winter months?

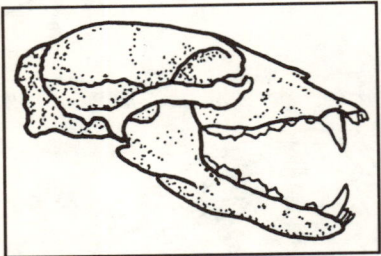

The largest and most powerful North American predators are bears. During the summer, bears eat large amounts of berries, insects and fish to prepare for the coming winter. In October, bears look for or dig dens where they can spend the winter. Bears sleep through much of the winter but do not truly hibernate. They may wake up and look around outside their den. Some may even eat. Females give birth to one or two cubs in their den in January or February. Bears become active and leave their dens in April. Bears are omnivorous: they eat anything. Bears are especially hungry when they leave their den. They my scavenge for the carcasses of animals that died during the winter or may kill weak, sickly animals. This is one of nature's ways of making sure that only strong, healthy animals survive.

There are two species of bears in the Yellowstone region: The black bear and the grizzly bear.

Black bears can be light brown to black in color, 6 feet long and weigh 400 pounds. They are found in nearly every region of North America. Both cubs and adult black bears climb trees. In this region, black bears have learned that humans bring food with them. It is a mistake to feed any bear. Feeding bears allows them close contact with humans which is very dangerous.

Grizzly bears are larger than black bears. They may be 7 feet long, weigh up to 900 pounds and have a hump on their back. Grizzlies have longer light brown to dark brown fur. Older bears may have silver-tipped fur. Adult grizzlies do not climb trees and may appear to be slow, easy going animals. In truth, grizzly bears are much faster than they look. Grizzlies can be very unpredictable and dangerously aggressive. Grizzly bears avoid humans.

You can also tell these two bears apart by their tracks. Black bears have claw marks directly in front of the toe marks. Grizzlies have longer paw prints with claw marks 2 to 4 inches in front of the toe marks. This paw print is from an average size adult grizzly. Large isn't it?

Bears have only one natural enemy: PEOPLE. Our ever growing population has moved into many of the areas that were once home to the grizzly bear. Today, there are less than 1000 grizzly bears in the lower 48 United States.

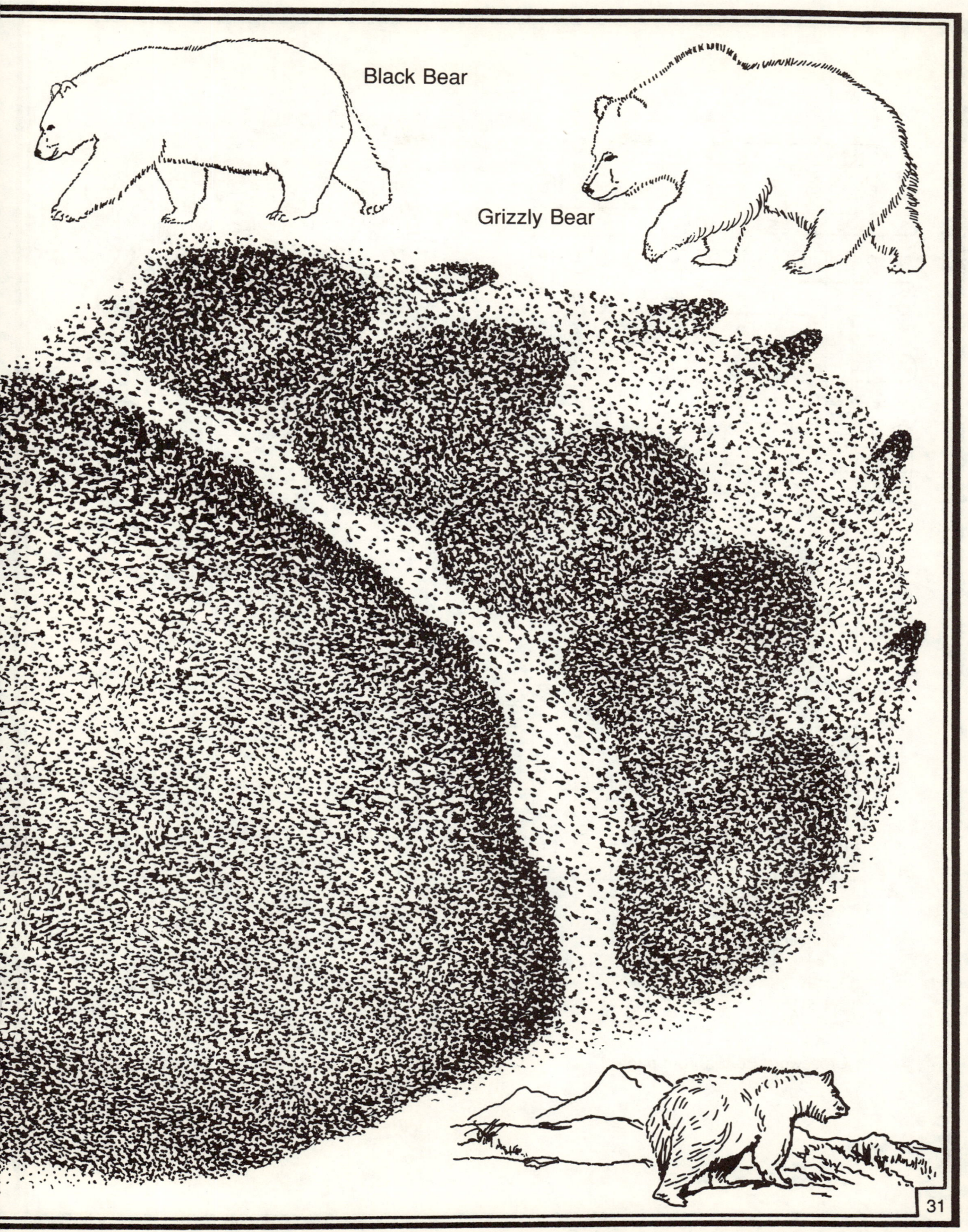

Black Bear

Grizzly Bear

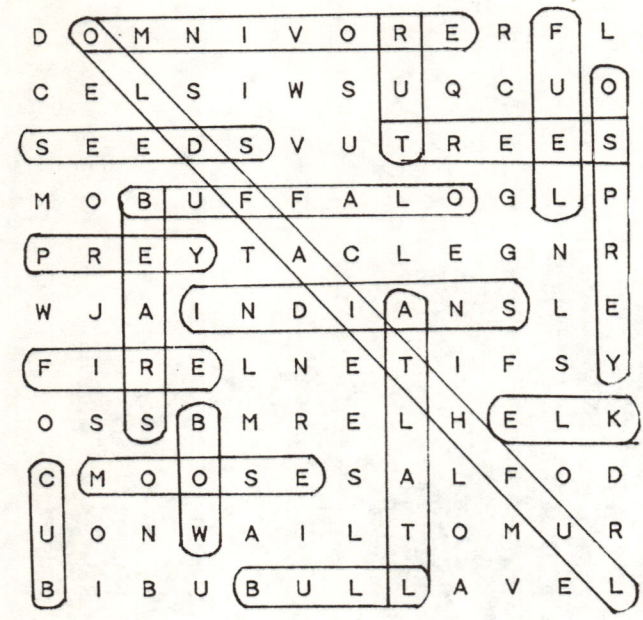

Wordsearch from page 11

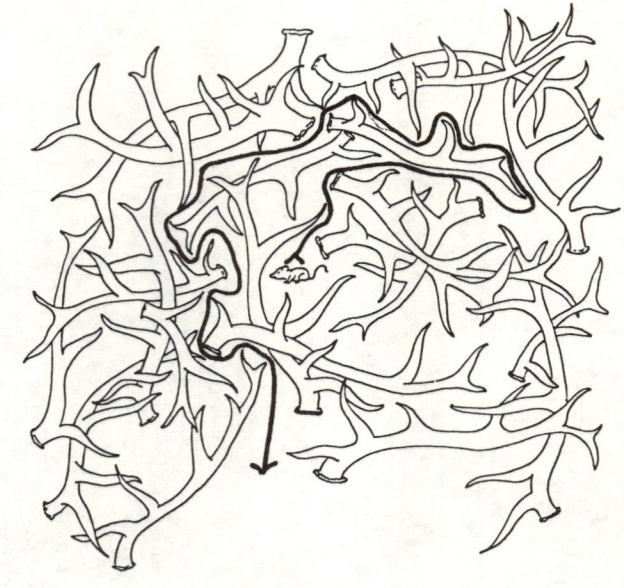

Maze from page 15

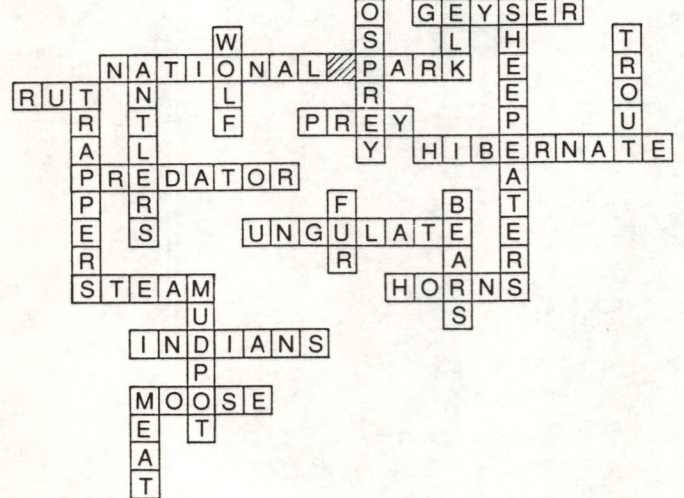

Crossword Puzzle from page 27

VOLCANO

GRIZZLY

BISON

LIGHTNING

FURS

SPEAR

PREDATORS

WYOMING

OUR EARTH'S ENVIRONMENT

Riddle Gram from page 28